JOYFUL, LOV.
ENLIGHTEN~ ~~~ ~~~~~~~ ~~
CHAN-DO
MADDY ☺

Bullet-Proof Belief

How to achieve every goal you set without fail

Maddy M

* THANK YOU, KIND SOUL, CHAN-DO

Bullet-Proof Belief: how to achieve every goal without fail

Text and illustrations copyright © 2011 Maddy M

First published in United Kingdom in 2011 by Maddy M

Disclaimer

Acknowledgments

To my mentors and coaches including the legendary Anthony Robbins, incredible Joseph McClendon III, top mental-toughness trainer Steve Siebold, the radio guy Wayne Kelly and writing coach/editor Tina Bettison.

To my dear friends who believe in me, genuinely care and motivate me including Hina H, Rachel L, Sonal B, Ameeta B, Vibhuti L, Jaspal S, Paul J, and Viral D.

To my inner-self and my body which has guided me and has been with me every minute of learning, adversity, growing and creating this book.

To the Universe for connecting me with great people and opportunities.

To all the authors, speakers and organizers of all the personal development books, seminars, workshops and courses I have read and attended.

To all my clients who gave me the opportunity to make a difference and to learn and grow.

And to everyone who has been part of my journey so far.

Foreword

I am going to share some basics of life which I have learned and implemented very successfully in my own life. These philosophies have been followed by every successful person and their roots can also be found in ancient wisdom.

I have attended many life-success and personal development seminars from the best in the world and what I am going to share is the summary of my learning. I have experimented, applied and lived these myself and my clients have benefited from it.

Along my journey I came across the story of the two wolves (which I'll share with you in chapter 1). For me this simple story sums up our internal battle – the battle between our resourceful beliefs and our limiting beliefs. It summed up the battle that raged within me and around me between the positive and negative beliefs I held about myself and the beliefs that others (parents, family, teachers) held about me. For too long the 'evil' wolf was feasting and the 'good' wolf went hungry!

However, I learned that there are ways of feeding the 'good' wolf and when I started to do that great things started to happen in my life:

The 'mess' started to untangle. It felt like I received answers to the 'puzzle' called life. My quest and hunger to know more of 'how life works', and how to live a life with more happiness, more peace, more satisfaction, began to be fulfilled.

I connected to my inner-self (which is also called the process of 'self-realisation').

I became curious like a child and started exploring all the resources I could to gain more knowledge – inspirational & spiritual seminars, books, videos, articles, audios, movies, forums & communities on the internet, courses etc.

I became more health conscious because I started looking at my body parts as precious and felt gifted.

I started enjoying music, dancing on my own and singing out loud!

I started becoming more relaxed and alive with a sense of well being through my whole body. And I started to sleep better (very important!).

Yes, it is possible for you to design and live the life of your dreams and my aim for this book is to make you aware of the elements required for a successful and fulfilled life. The most important of which is a bullet-proof self belief, because that underpins *everything*. You need to believe totally in yourself and your abilities if you are going to achieve anything. Success in any area of life begins in your mind. It's the 'inner' work you need to do first. A hidden lack of self belief is usually what sabotages our efforts.

'Far better is it to dare mighty things, to win glorious triumphs, even though checked by failure... than to rank with those poor spirits who neither enjoy much nor suffer much, because they live in a gray twilight that knows not victory nor defeat.'
~ Theodore Roosevelt

You don't know what you don't know. While reading this book some of you may think 'what is this guy talking about' and that's understandable because most of us are unaware of these realities about life. Our minds have been programmed otherwise. I can assure you this works. It will be worth the investment.

I would like to thank you for sparing time and congratulate you for taking action, by reading this book. I would love to receive your comments and suggestions.

Maddy M.

Maddy M
Bullet-Proof Belief Coach, Speaker, Author
Britain's Happiest Young Man

www.bulletproofbelief.com

Table of Contents

Maddy M - the hungry wolf 2

Life in the 21st Century 10

What they didn't teach you about success and happiness 15

Your biggest barrier to success and happiness.. 20

You were programmed to fail... 25

Do you think like the successful do? 34

The voice in your head.. 37

Emotions - what are they making you do 43

Ten things the most successful, happiest and healthiest people believe in

and do 47

Practical tips and techniques to make your life better............................. 56

Congratulations!.. 65

Next Steps with Maddy M.. 68

Maddy M

Maddy M - the hungry wolf

First, the story:

One evening an old Cherokee told his grandson about a battle that goes on inside people.

He said, 'My son, the battle is between two 'wolves' inside us all. One is *Evil*. It is anger, envy, jealousy, sorrow, regret, greed, arrogance, self-pity, guilt, resentment, inferiority, lies, false pride, superiority, and ego.

The other is *Good*. It is joy, peace, love, hope, serenity, humility, kindness, benevolence, empathy, generosity, truth, compassion and faith.'

The grandson thought about it for a minute and then asked his grandfather: 'Which wolf wins?'

The old Cherokee simply replied, *'The one you feed.'*

My Name is 'Madhur' but people call me 'Maddy'. I grew up in a semi-developed town in the outskirts of Delhi. This town was one of the top three crime areas in India. In my illustrious neighbourhood there was no electricity for up to 12 hours every day. The drinking water was deemed undrinkable by the World Health Organization; there were no water filters and the water was supplied for just an hour a day - if there was an electric supply. There was no air-conditioning when it was 45 degrees and no room or water heaters when it was 5 degrees.

In my town there were no health and safety laws. In our house, the food was cooked in a clay oven or on a kerosene stove throughout my childhood. We did not have the privilege of having access to a telephone, a washing machine or other modern household appliances.

I had no soft toys or electronic gadgets and I was not given any pocket money so I had to fish marbles out of the drain in order to play with other children.

My family was very religious. There was an hour's prayer in the morning and another hour in the evening with visits to the temple as well. We lived in a six bedroom house but there were three families and three couples living in that six bedroom house; all of them were my extended family.

I was never hugged, kissed or praised by my parents because they believed that beating your child was the road to your child's success. The mindset of my family was a mixture of miserliness along with working class and some middle class beliefs. On top of all this my family discriminated against the poor and darker skinned people and that influenced my relations with others then and later in life. Abuse (physical, sexual, mental) was rife in the community I lived in and the close proximity of humans living so tightly together.

I tell you this not for sympathy, but because when you understand my background you can also understand why the 'good' wolf went very hungry for many years. Poverty and deprivation is not just about poor living standards, many suffer from emotional deprivation just because they grew up in a time or place where feeding the 'good' wolf was considered soft or weak, and the way to motivate your child was the stick not the carrot.

My story is not unique in the world, but I found a way to change the probable ending and to rewrite my predicted future, and that is what I want to help you to do too.

Not surprisingly I was a below average student. I was not interested in what they had to teach me. Inevitably I was bullied. So... what were my prospects? What could a boy from such an environment expect, or indeed hope for? Hope is our birthright; and hope, fortunately, springs eternal in the human breast.

English is my third language. I did not speak the Indian version of proper English until I was 22 years old. My relatives who lived in the city referred to me as a 'villager'. This was not a compliment! (Incidentally when I finally reached the UK, I was unable to understand or communicate properly for almost 2 years!) Despite my academic inadequacies, my parents had ambitions for me. Their chief, rather unrealistic, hope was that I would be a doctor of medicine! Or a telecoms engineer.

But I could not, for love nor money, get a place at any university in or around Delhi. I was told this gave a bad name to the family. My poor achievements meant that everyone lost hope in me and I was told that my fate was, horror of horrors, to live a working class life. But I am a fighter and against the odds, I confounded them by enrolling for a degree at the Open University.

Despite working hard at my course, the pressure from my parents continued. The mind games they played reinforced in them (and often in me) their notions that I was a failure and would never be able to lead a contented and abundant life. My already low self-esteem plummeted.

An additional pressure was that the extended family in India thinks it is their right to chip in with their negative forecasts and expectations. I was forced to be more religious than I wished and to do what astrologers and priests told me. I became bowed down by the limiting, negative beliefs of the very society in which I lived.

Boy, was that 'evil' wolf having a feast! But still there remained a driving force within me to prove my worth and to prove them wrong! The 'good' wolf was starving but he was determined to survive!

So I did something that surprised them all. Talk about burning your bridges! At the age of 23 with my frustration steadily increasing, I decided to leave my country for good. I took out a loan of, what was for me, the enormous sum of $8,000! This was for a diploma in customer service management in a place called Nottingham. 'Where is Nottingham?' I thought. I had also managed to save, by leading a non-existent social life for eight years, the princely sum of £200 for living expenses.

Now, I did not really know what the UK was. I knew the names London, Britain and England and now I knew of Nottingham. All I really knew was that I desperately wanted to leave India and migrate to a developed country. I was flying to London - I was going to England!!

This was a period of many 'firsts' for me - first time away from home, first visa, first time at an airport and on an airplane. A lot for our village boy to deal with!

My arrival in the UK was a huge cultural and technological shock. I did not know anyone in the UK. My £200 saved over eight years lasted me for less than eight days - quite an achievement!

Throughout my diploma course I was forced to work part time to survive. For the first three months I worked as a dishwasher at a restaurant. That was a big dent in my self-esteem.

For the first 11 months in the UK I could afford only two meals a day. At one time I was doing two part-time jobs a day. Then I landed a job in a call centre and this sustained me until the course finished.

The added pressure and challenge was the knowledge that no one in India supported me, or believed in me. My parents predicted that I would return a failure, my tail between my legs, having wasted the money I had borrowed. I should point out that the loan of $8,000 in India represented two years salary for an accountant or doctor. But...I managed to pay off that loan after only 2 years in England! And then left my job in the call centre and burnt my bridges again!!

I borrowed a further $9,000 to pursue a specialist course in Computer Networking in London. Whilst studying for this course I continued to live on the fringes of society, constantly borrowing from very good friends just to get by. There were drugs, alcohol, gambling and prostitution present in the house I lived in, a constant and depressing backdrop to this period.

I was fortunate or unfortunate enough, on the 7th July 2005, to be on one of the tube trains which was found to have a bomb, (unexploded)!! Was luck on my side or just teasing me?

And each year the application for the Visa extension was ever more stressful! It seemed so hard to swim against the current towards the open sea. I sometimes felt I was merely treading water.

I asked myself: had that 'village' boy, back in India, been foolish to have his dreams and hopes? Was he heading out of the frying pan and into the fire?

Then, after all that studying, debt and hardship, in August 2005 I got a good Job with British Telecom in Sheffield. I once again applied for my visa and received one of the 'Highly Skilled' variety! I also joined the British Red Cross as a volunteer.

YES! Life was getting better now that I had a full time job. My confidence and self esteem grew and flourished. The news came from India that the parents and the extended family were pleased; they were prepared to rejoice with me in my achievements and good fortune. I paid off all my loans, opened a savings account, and could afford better food, luxuries and clothes. A lesson had been well learned about life's possibilities! My 'good' wolf was getting a few morsels at last.

But as time passed, nagging doubts grew. There had to be more to life than financial security and physical well being. I had anticipated that attaining worldly success would bring me the happiness I longed for. When achieving this success failed to deliver happiness, I sought it elsewhere.

In 2007 I attended my first motivational seminar and read my first self-help book in 2008 and then attended and read many more led and written by the best in the world.

My previously religious mindset changed to a more spiritual one. A transformation gradually occurred and my beliefs began to change. Life was full of possibilities! I could plan my own destiny and get rid of limiting beliefs... I felt I was exploring and becoming connected to myself. At last my mind was clear and positive.

Alongside my full time job I completed courses in life coaching, NLP (Neuro Linguistic Programming), hypnotherapy and psychology. And I have attempted to implement the knowledge in myself... I have made an effort to

- **change my limiting beliefs**
- become aware and take control of my **thoughts and emotions**
- forgive myself and others,
- start loving myself,
- be thankful for all that I have - even for the pain I had, in the past
- and smile more often

I have studied successful leaders and have noted their strengths and techniques and attempted to model them.

With all this new study, I began to write like crazy. I used to wake up in the middle of the night and start writing. There was a flow of inspiration and power from within me. And I started writing about attaining Happiness and Peace in the 21st century.

So, professionally, I had achieved a level of success every Indian parent would like their child to have reached, a level most of the top graduates from India would want to have reached; and I was doing pretty well by British standards too! I worked for a prestigious organisation, earning 100 times more than I used to five years ago!

Do you sense the familiar aroma of burning bridges? You are right to! I took another big step and quit my day job to fulfil my passion.

In the past many people commented that I was 'too happy and peppy for my own good. That I didn't take my responsibilities seriously enough'. But I always knew my natural joy and energy were, and are, my greatest strengths. I am well placed and on the brink of achieving my dream.

I had an option to buy a house, start a business (franchisee) or even invest in share market but I chose to invest my savings in myself. It was a tough decision, involved many calculations and I had to deal with fear of financial security and fear of failure. Since 2007 I have invested over $43,000 in personal development. My colleagues and friends thought I had lost the plot when I disclosed that. ☺

I decided to learn from the best mentors in the world. My learning continues and I am hungry to know more about life, and understand why we do what we do. I am constantly attempting to get my hands on more tools and techniques through which I can live a better life and share my knowledge with others so that they can too.

I have had one-to-one coaching with the best mental toughness coach in the world and had a personal life coach for a year. I am a certified Hypnotherapist, NLP practitioner and have studied life coaching at three different institutes. I have also taken a course in psychology at the University of Oxford.

I am thankful for all that I have. Happiness, joy, contentment, peace and gratitude are part of my daily life now. My good wolf is fed and flourishing. The 'evil' wolf is now the one who is hungry.

And so I would like to share with you some of the amazing things I have learnt on this journey. Some things you might be familiar with and some things may be as much a surprise to you as they were to me. Either way, your 'good' wolf will be grateful for the nourishment, and ultimately so will you.

'I am not a teacher, only a fellow traveller of whom you asked the way. I pointed ahead – ahead of myself as well as you.' ~ George Bernard Shaw

Life in the 21st Century

Are you living or surviving or fighting or coping?

With advanced technology this is the most comfortable and easy life humans have lived in the past few centuries but mentally the 21st century seems to be the worst time to live. We are more stressed mentally than we have ever been. Why?

We are facing a mental health pandemic – all of us suffering from poor mental health at some point in our lives. We think of mental health being something that affects other people. But actually it affects everyone. The World Health Organisation defines mental health as 'a state of well-being in which every individual realizes his or her own potential, can cope with the normal stresses of life, can work productively and fruitfully, and is able to make a contribution to her or his community. It's a state of complete physical, mental and social well-being and not merely the absence of disease or infirmity.'

How many of us would say that we feel constantly in a 'state of complete physical, mental and social well-being'? Or that we even achieve it some of the time?

Depression is increasingly common – and can strike anyone at anytime. By the year 2020, depression will be the second most common health problem in the world. And that's just one type of mental health issue.

'Mental health problems do not affect three of four out of every five persons, but one out of one' ~ *Dr. William Menninger*

Stress is the most common issue and is ignored by many of us. Research has proven that negative emotions associated with stress such as anxiety, fear, lack of forgiveness, anger, envy etc (all those 'evil wolf' traits!) can cause the release of chemicals (neuropeptides released by the brain) that could lead to poor digestion, irregular heartbeat, high blood pressure and inflammation of the body parts, ulcer, pains, skin diseases, IBS, panic attacks. And this can lead to major illnesses like cancer, depression, diabetes, heart disease. Knowing that why would you want to allow stress to take over?

PsychoNeuroImmunology suggests that hormones such as adrenaline and cortisol (helpful when required) are released in unexpected amounts when a person experiences negative emotions. Such chemicals weaken the immune system. They become toxic for our body and can cause our bodies to create toxic cells which cause dis-ease.

Can you imagine all the diseases or illnesses you are prone to if your immune system is weak or disabled?

On the contrary, positive emotions such as laughter, fulfilment, contentment etc. can make the brain release chemicals which can strengthen the immune system and help an individual to prevent and/or heal cancer and other illnesses. What a relief!

'People are about as happy as they make up their minds to be.' ~ *Abraham Lincoln*

People these days are so busy in the rat race of professional growth and earning money that they forget to allocate time and energy for experiencing these positive emotions; finding time and energy for their loved ones, for their peace of mind, for relaxation, for hobbies, for travelling, for fitness, to connect with themselves, to be thankful for what they have, to even celebrate their achievements!

A birthday in the family, anniversaries, public holidays and in some cases vacations - are these the only days when we must feel happy?

Facebook now has more than 500,000,000 users and has started measuring how happy or satisfied with life the citizens of a nation are as part of the

Gross National Happiness Movement. You can see the graph for your country by clicking: http://apps.facebook.com/gnh_index

Their data is drawn from the use of what they term positive and negative words posted on Facebook updates. The graphs show a sad picture. Either happiness has become an occasional thing for most of people (users are mostly happy only around public holidays) or we use Facebook for complaining more than we do for spreading our happiness among our friends. Have we lost the happiness habit?

Sure we all have problems, such as:

1) Finances – in debt, just getting by, no savings

2) Physical Health – overweight, pains,

3) Relationships – living like housemates, occasional love making, lack of time/commitment

4) Mental Health –

   a) Self – low self-esteem, negative self-image, lack of confidence,

   b) Emotions – stress, anxiety, fears, frustration, guilt, worry, anger, depression, envy, jealousy,

And we deal with these problems in a variety of ways (some more crippling than others):

Smoking, alcohol, emotional eating, drugs, self-harm, pain killers, emotional spending abusing others, getting a pet, producing a baby, becoming a perfectionist to prove our worth, becoming a victim/passive… and a lot of people fool themselves by distracting themselves, ignoring their problems and by suppressing their emotions!

And what are the consequences of using such coping mechanisms? *More problems!!*

Unfortunately most of the treatments or solutions available to us deal with the effects of the problem not the cause. Despite billions of dollars (or £pounds) being poured into the health sector, much of it is directed at treating symptoms not at finding the root cause of the problem. But we don't have to wait for governments to change their focus. **We can start to change it for ourselves and within ourselves.**

We can't solve the problem by focusing on and worrying about the problem itself (feeding the 'evil' wolf!). We need to focus on what is positive in our lives and find the solutions from there.

The following chapters will help you do just that: understand your thinking that is creating problems in your life and changing your thinking to create solutions and find a better life. There are questions at the end of each chapter which will help you explore yourself and your thoughts.

'No problem can be solved from the same level of consciousness that created it.'
~ Albert Einstein

Explore yourself

How many times a day do you use these words or feel happy, I can, joyful, possible, thankful, confident, peaceful, delighted, excellent, cheerful, fantastic, proud, love, great, celebrate and enjoyed/enjoying?

Versus

How many times a day do you use these words or feel stressed, anxious, frustrated, need a break, f**king hell, angry, blaming yourself/life/others, depressed, worried, unlucky, sad, fear/fearful, not good enough, rubbish, sh*t, thoughts of lack or scarcity, negative assumptions or doubts?

What does this tell you about the quality of life you are living right now?

What's the logic in having a prestigious job or an established business but lack of emotional fulfilment, physical health issues and/or relationship problems? Is your life balanced?

Why can't we be as happy and lively every evening as we are on a Friday?

Do we need a tag/label for a day of the year to celebrate it? Why do we celebrate our birth only once a year?

Your Notes

What they didn't teach you about success and happiness

Most of us are NOT aware of the facts of life which affect us every single minute!

Have you ever wondered why things don't happen the way they should? Why is it so difficult to live a life of our dreams? Why so some people seem to be lucky while most of us live a life of mediocrity? Some people seem to be happy all day long, are wealthy and enjoy their life more than the majority of us. Why?

A sad truth is that most of us don't know what we really believe! We don't know how we operate. We don't know what is holding us back. We don't know why we do what we do. Why do we like some things and dislike others? What makes us decide right and wrong? To learn how to read and write we go to school, to learn a profession we often go to a college or university, to learn any technical skills we get trained. Why don't we learn about the mental health (our thoughts, emotions and beliefs) which affects every minute of our lives? Why don't we study and set goals for our relationships? Why don't we make an effort to learn about the ways to create a healthy self-esteem? Where is the school for learning positive mental health? (Actually it is right here – read on!)

Parenting, emotional wellness, love making… do we assume we know it all or we let our lives run on autopilot?

Today, the word 'success' is understood as having lots of money, material things and/or fame but that's success in only one or two areas of life. What about the other areas? What about our health, happiness and relationships?

Areas of Life

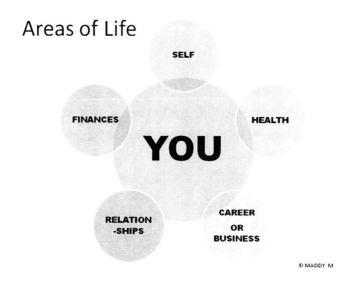

Remember, you DO need to work on and give your time and energy to your relationships, physical health, personal development, mental health, spirituality and fun and recreation in order to succeed, **or else you will have the money but no love, joy, peace or fulfilment.**

Money is a must. We all need it to survive, BUT it is no substitute for love, joy, peace and fulfilment. We need these to ensure we thrive as well as survive.

We are born with everything we need to be happy often, to be rich, to have a loving soul mate, to have a healthy body, to be confident. But no one taught us how to access these powers and abilities from within us. No one taught us the psychology of success, of happiness, of love. We can learn it though, and it is never too late to do so.

'It is remarkable how much mediocrity we live with, surrounding ourselves with daily reminders that the average is acceptable. Our world suffers from terminal normality. Take a moment to assess all of the things around you that promote your being 'average'. These are the things that keep you powerless to go beyond a 'limit' you arbitrarily set for yourself.' ~ Stewart Emery

We are all born in a world full of illusion, people sleepwalking. May be that is why ancient wisdom and the spiritual gurus alive ask us to 'awaken'. Self-realisation, self-awakening, self-awareness takes us to the peak of positive emotions and full control on our lives.

'If most of us remain ignorant of ourselves, it is because self-knowledge is painful and we prefer the pleasures of illusion.' ~ Aldous Huxley

Explore yourself

Why you do what you do? (Your decisions, choices, dislike, like, procrastination, right or wrong, things you know are bad or harmful for you but still do them)

Why you are where you are in your life? (Success or failure in each area of life, depressed or happy, fit or overweight, in a loving relationship or not, low self-esteem or high)

What is stopping you from living the life of your dreams? (Things you wish to have/own in every area of your life but you don't have them)

Your Notes

Your biggest barrier to success and happiness

Most of us are victims of self-sabotage (unconsciously).

That's right. Most of us are getting in our own way to earning more money, getting fit, feeling happy, loving ourselves and others!!

Our relationship with ourselves is the most important relationship in our lives and if that relationship isn't love-full, joy-full and peace-full - if we aren't our own best friends - then we must not expect to live a success-full and fulfilled life.

Your opinion about yourself (i.e. how capable you are, how much success and happiness you can achieve, what you deserve and your self-worth) affects your relationships, profession, health, performance and your self-esteem.

Most of us don't love ourselves. We keep giving love to others but rarely to ourselves! And that is just keeping your 'good' wolf hungry!

Think of how many times do you say 'I love you' to others? And now count the no. of times you say it to yourself?

Do you feel sorry for yourself? Misery won't help you make your life better. Successful people have described self-pity as poison for life and a barrier to success.

The questions you ask when you feel hopeless, such as:

Why me? Why my life? Why does this happen to me?

Who answers them? What answer do you get?

You may have had bad experiences during childhood, may be your parents divorced, you were bad at academic subjects, you lived in poverty, you were abused....

So what?

Are there people who had similar problems in their past or even worse problems than yours who are now rich, happy, love-full, confident and thankful?

Yes! There are many examples, including me.

'All blame is a waste of time. No matter how much fault you find with another, and regardless of how much you blame him, it will not change you. The only thing blame does is to keep the focus off you when you are looking for external reasons to explain your unhappiness or frustration. You may succeed in making another feel guilty about something by blaming him, but you won't succeed in changing whatever it is about you that is making you unhappy.' ~ Dr. Wayne Dyer

Do you tell yourself: I will be happy when I do/achieve X Y Z?

If you think that you will start enjoying life or you will be happy or proud 'when' or 'if only' you have a million dollars in your bank, or once you buy a nice car or the day you move into your dream house or the day you have a degree or the day you have a perfect soul mate or the day you have your own business or a high designation job... then you are missing out. You don't have to wait. **Happiness, peace, love and pride come from within. You have the choice of feeling happy anytime and anywhere you wish.**

'If you keep running away from yourself then be warned that love, joy, peace and fulfilment will keep running away from you!' ~ Maddy M

Most of us learn to evaluate our self-worth by comparing and competing which is why we have a tendency to compare ourselves with our friends, co-workers, family members and so on. Sadly, this is the root cause of much of the emotional pain that we experience.

Because most of us have a low self-belief and self-esteem (includes self image, confidence, love, worth) we are addicted to the approval of others. We have a fear of being judged or rejected. We are, often, worried about what 'they' will think about us. Our happiness and worth is dependent on 'their' approval.

'If you compare yourself to others, you may become vain and bitter; for always there will be greater and lesser persons than yourself.' ~ *Max Ehrmann*

Explore yourself

Do you think you are unlucky?

Do you think no one can ever truly love you?

Do you think you don't deserve a happy life?

Do you think you can never be rich?

Do you think your fate is to be abandoned?

Have you accepted unhappiness as your fate?

Do you think life can't always be happy?

(Chapters 5 and 6 will help you understand why you think this way and give you ways to change your thinking.)

How many times a day do you say/think negative things about yourself and/or your life?

Vs

How many times a day do you appreciate yourself and/or recognise your achievements?

How many times a day you blame your fate and/or others for all the problems in your life?

Whom do you hold responsible for your life?

Your Notes

Your	Impacts On your	Which affect
Beliefs **Thoughts** **Emotions**	Attitude Decisions Actions Results	Finances Health Career / Business Relationships Self Esteem

You were programmed to fail

Most of us live by someone else's script; like a pre-programmed robot.

Is it the physical disability which stops people? NO.

There are disabled people who are scientists, motivational speakers, marathon runners, engineers...

Is it lack of education which stops people? NO.

A lot of billionaires and multi-millionaires don't have a degree.

Is it lack of finances which stops people? NO.

Many successful entrepreneurs (including billionaires) weren't born rich or lost all their assets and were in debt at some point.

Most of the people who attend money-making courses don't make much money. Why?

Most of the people who attend motivational seminars slip back to their comfort zone after a week or two. Why?

Goal setting or New Year resolutions don't last for long. Why?

Why is it?

It's because of our BELIEFS.

Your beliefs are the blueprint of your reality. It is referred to as a script or a life plan in Transactional Analysis (an integrative approach to psychology and psychotherapy).

'A belief is assuming something to be true, to be a fact. A belief is not caused, it is created by choice. A belief about a thing's existence is not the same as its existence.'
~ Bruce Di Marsico

If you don't have the successful career or business that provides the money, fulfilment and freedom, the loving and joyful relationships you desire, the ideal body shape or weight, high self-esteem or self confidence, it's all because of your beliefs!!

Unfortunately most of our intense beliefs are NOT created by us consciously! They are someone else's beliefs which we act upon and defend! **Very few of us examine our beliefs critically. We unconsciously live our lives with beliefs that were, and are, programmed or conditioned into us by others** (parents, teachers, family, bosses, even friends and colleagues).

It's not your fault. And to an extent it isn't theirs either! Most of the people you rely on and learn from including your parents, school/college teachers, community leaders, GPs (medical Doctors), finance consultants, bank managers, don't know about these facts of life either!!

'In medical school, we have a hundred classes that teach us how to fight off death and not one lesson in how to go on living.' ~ Dr. Meredith Grey

Beliefs start forming the day you were born (some studies reveal they can even be created while you were in the womb). Since then your mind has been recording everything (images, sounds, feelings, tastes and smells) and storing it at a subconscious level.

Various studies show different age groups for this process. In general, the first five to seven years are the most critical for belief formation. The process continues until 15-18. During and after that, usually, we keep repeating what we have been programmed for and form new beliefs with our experiences or verify our old beliefs each time we get a reference to prove them right.

Warning! Our subconscious mind is NOT rational i.e. it can't evaluate whether a belief is good for you or not. It just stores whatever you allow in. Your subconscious will just keep feeding that 'evil' wolf if that is the food you are giving it.

Those beliefs/programs/scripts/blueprints which were created in the first few years of your life (when you didn't even have the ability to question what your mind was recording) are still there and affecting your feelings, attitudes, decisions and actions every day.

Teachers, parents, celebrities and other leaders are, usually, children's role models. If most of these people don't know the power of beliefs, the basic emotional needs and how the life can be made happier, peaceful and love-full, then what are the kids going to learn?

Parents or guardians make us live as per their values, rules and beliefs. Most of them don't know unconsciously they are programming a child's mind. Even when we have grown up and left home, we continue to live 'their' beliefs and perform up to the expectations they had of us during our childhood.

We keep doing what they wanted us to do and keep on believing that all that they told us was right. And we rarely question those beliefs!

This programming is the biggest reason why we have low self-esteem/self-confidence/self-love/self-image; why we can't achieve much and sabotage our success unconsciously; why we don't feel fulfilled; why some of us are passive; why we become perfectionists; why we never experience complete peace of mind; why others are more important than our self, which makes us feel guilty irrationally, which tells us we aren't good enough and the list goes on...

Negative programming of mind, repetition with intense negative emotions or abuse, blame and reminders of the mistakes a child has made, comparison with siblings or their friends, and then labelling or telling the child how stupid, doomed, bad, a failure, a loser, useless, ugly (or any other abusive words) he/she is, makes the child believe it and unconsciously the child keeps believing, living and proving the negative labels, given to her/him, all her/his life.

Most of us were programmed for lack and limitations.

Hopefully this tells you why you are the way you are! The good news is you don't have to continue believing it!

Learned behaviour
Learned behaviour can be defined as the behaviour we learn through our environment.

If the kids see their parents drinking or smoking often then they may create a belief that these stimulants are a part of life and it's ok to consume.

If the kids have heard their parents saying Friday/Saturday night out is fun and the kids see them getting drunk and using positive words for their experience then kids will tend to do the same.

If the kids have seen their parents fighting/arguing/abusing each other, or if one parent is abusing or controlling the other, then what type of beliefs will they create around relationships?

I know many university students who use stimulants for social anxiety or they have a belief to 'enjoy' life as much as they can now. Where do they learn all this?

In Britain, kids are programmed to relate negative emotions and abusive words with rain. Without thinking about it consciously the grown up kids then use the same language and add misery to their lives!

Can you change or control the weather? If not then accept it and reprogram your reaction. Try being grateful for the rain even, some countries need it so badly and don't get any.

What are Doubts? Assumptions? Fears? Worries? Limitations? Excuses?

They are our beliefs and exist only in our mind and they have a negative effect on our feelings, decisions and results in every area of our lives including our physical health!

Are you aware of the term 'placebo'? Patients are given inactive substance like a sugar pill, distilled water or saline solution rather than the real drugs. Patients still improve merely because of their **belief** about the effect of the medicine!

When you say something like 'I have a bad memory', 'I am not/never organised', 'I have a bad habit of ___', 'I have been doing ___ for years', you are reinforcing that habit/behaviour/belief in your mind and so you continue to do/be the same.

Who programmed or continuously programs us?

- Parents/Guardian
- Extended family/Relatives
- Media – TV, Radio, Newspapers, Magazines, Books, Internet (especially news, songs, movies)
- Politicians, Religious or Community leaders and other authority figures in life
- Teachers, Friends, Classmates, Colleagues and other people whom you spend time with
- Advertising banners, posters, t-shirts, stickers, mugs etc

And we do it to ourselves!

Warning! Be aware of whom you spend time with or what do you read, watch or listen.

Have you seen the movie or the read the book called The Secret?

Many personal development speakers, teachers and life-coaches suggest their clients should 'look in the mirror and say good things' about themselves, some suggest affirmations, some prescribe applying the Law of Attraction. These are techniques that work if you **truly believe** those good things or affirmations. But if you say them without believing them, nothing will change. Without dealing with your underlying limiting beliefs, it's impossible to achieve success and/or happiness.

'It is that constant daily programming you receive that determines your mindset. And it is your mindset that determines your eventual level of achievement in everything you do.' ~ Randy Gage

Explore yourself

How many beliefs have you got, which work against you?

How many hours of negative/limiting programming do you have each day versus reading self-help books, attending seminars and positive self-talk/affirmations?

Today why would you believe the negative labels you were given at 13? Have you not learnt more, experienced more or done more since then?

So if you aren't at the same level as you were at 13 then why would you have the same self-image/worth/confidence?

If I ask you to write 50 achievements of your life, what is the first thought that comes to your mind? Usually people say 'I can't even think of 10' because their head is full of negative beliefs about them and they are always blaming themselves for all the mistakes and failures from the past. People usually come up with more than 50 when asked to change their focus and rethink! So go ahead and see how many achievements you can think of.

Your Notes

Do you think like the successful do?

Most of us, everyday, have a lot more negative or disempowering thoughts than positive ones.

Remember the two wolves?

Here's a reminder of the story:

One evening an old Cherokee told his grandson about a battle that goes on inside people. He said, 'My son, the battle is between two 'wolves' inside us all. One is 'Evil'. It is anger, envy, jealousy, sorrow, regret, greed, arrogance, self-pity, guilt, resentment, inferiority, lies, false pride, superiority, and ego.

The other is 'Good'. It is joy, peace, love, hope, serenity, humility, kindness, benevolence, empathy, generosity, truth, compassion and faith.'

The grandson thought about it for a minute and then asked his grandfather: 'Which wolf wins?'

The old Cherokee simply replied, 'The one you feed.'

Have you ever considered exploring what you focus on during your day? What type of thoughts cross your mind? Which of those thoughts are repetitive? Are they negative or positive? Which wolf are you feeding?

What do you think about yourself, others, your ability, about life in general, about what is possible in future and about the world as a whole?

If the answers to the questions above are more negative than positive, like most of us, then you may never be able to live the life of your dreams. WHY?

Because of this powerful fact which may surprise you or make you think...

Your thoughts become your physical reality!!

'We are what we think. All that we are arises with our thoughts. With our thoughts, we make the world.' ~ Buddha

We live in the world, of our thoughts, all day long. The amount of happiness, success, love, peace and fulfilment you experience and achieve depends on the nature and quality of your thoughts.

Either you must control your thoughts or the outside forces will control them and be warned that the outside forces are usually negative (limiting, fearful, worry, doubts, disempowering...)

Control your thoughts, focus on what's important and you may get better results.

'A man's mind may be likened to a garden, which may be intelligently cultivated or allowed to run wild; but whether cultivated or neglected, it must, and will, bring forth. If no useful seeds are put into it, then an abundance of useless weed seeds will fall therein, and will continue to produce their kind. Just as a gardener cultivates his plot, keeping it free from weeds, and growing the flowers and fruits which he requires, so may a man tend the garden of his mind, weeding out all the wrong, useless, and impure thoughts, and cultivating toward perfection the flowers and fruits of right, useful, and pure thoughts, By pursuing this process, a man sooner or later discovers that he is the master gardener of his soul, the director of his life.' ~ James Allen

It doesn't matter who you are, what your religion is, where you live, what your age is… this law is true for every human being:

The Law of Attraction also known as, 'success-consciousness', 'power of thought', 'like attracts like' or 'Law of Magnetism' **states that all of our thoughts, all the images in our minds, and all the emotions/feelings connected with our thoughts will sooner or later manifest as our reality**. The law of 'cause and effect', 'sow and reap', the law of 'intention' also give us a similar message.

Modern science has proved the law of attraction by the fundamentals of quantum physics. Ancient wisdom too consists of references which prove the above as true/fact. Every major religion has documented this in one form or other.

'What you resist, you attract, because you are powerfully focused on it with emotion. To change anything, go within and emit a new signal with your thoughts and feelings.'
~ Rhonda Byrne

Taking responsibility of your life and knowing the fact that you attract people and events in life is scary, isn't it?

Most people focus on what they don't want so they attract more of it in their lives. We must focus on what we do want.

Are you now thinking that is it your thinking which matters? Yes, that is all that matters to start with. Repetitive thoughts become beliefs.

Science is proving it now and the old spiritual books said it centuries ago that **negative thoughts are the primary source of all the internal and external diseases and illnesses!**

So feeding that 'evil' wolf isn't just making you feel bad emotionally, it can make you feel bad physically too. All the more reason to make your 'good' wolf stronger!

'The physical creation follows the mental, just as a building follows a blueprint. If you don't make a conscious effort to visualize who you are and what you want in life, then you empower other people and circumstances to shape you and your life by default.' ~
Dr. Stephen R. Covey

Explore yourself

What thoughts do you regularly think that feed your 'evil' wolf?

What thoughts could you think instead that would feed your 'good' wolf?

Your notes

The voice in your head

How you talk to yourself determines how you feel about yourself, and determines the actions you take.

All of us, all the time, talk to ourselves. We have a voice inside our head which we call 'self-talk' (also known as internal dialogue, self-suggestions, inner-critique etc.). It may be loud or silent and includes our conscious thoughts but the majority of it is our unconscious beliefs or assumptions.

It says things like – should I go to work today?; I'm hungry; I wonder what my kid is doing right now; wow that girl is attractive; I really like those shoes; oh I have a headache; maybe I should go to the shop later; I hope…; If only…; I wish…; What will they…; I am…; I can't…; Why me… I may… etc.

'I shouldn't have eaten that much! I'm so stupid. I'll never lose the weight to get into a swimsuit. I don't like myself in the mirror!'

I have a bad memory! I just know it won't work! I will never have any savings! I ain't good enough for this! My desk is always a mess! There is no way I can handle this! I can't say 'no' to people! I can't take it anymore! If only I had more time! S/he drives me mad! I hate my job! If only I had more money! I am unlucky! I am never organised! If only I had that degree! I am depressed!

Do YOU think things like this? These kind of thoughts or feelings are called negative self-talk (also known as self-defeating, self-blame, scarcity mindset, self-doubt). If someone else shouted at you with all the blames above, how would you react? Would it feel good? If someone said the above for your child, would you believe it?

Then WHY do you take this crap from yourself, from your own negative voice?

Another thing which is common is that many times the voice in our head isn't ours. It could be one of our parents, teachers, authority figures, partner, close friend or colleague… someone whose feedback/blame really mattered at the time we created that belief.

'The inner speech, your thoughts, can cause you to be rich or poor, loved or unloved, happy or unhappy, attractive or unattractive, powerful or weak.' ~ Ralph Charell

Well known psychologist, anxiety treatment specialist and author, Edmund J. Bourne, Ph.D, states that self-talk is so automatic and subtle you don't notice it or the effect it has on your moods and feelings. Anxious self-talk is typically irrational but almost always sounds like the truth. Negative self-talk perpetuates avoidance and can initiate or aggravate a panic attack.

In many situations, the only thing you can control is your own response. Changing self-talk from negative to positive is an excellent way to manage that response (rather than reacting badly with anger or snapping).

'Every waking moment we talk to ourselves about the things we experience. Our self-talk, the thoughts we communicate to ourselves, in turn controls the way we feel and act.' ~ John Lembo

Most of us are unaware of the words we use on a regular basis. We weren't taught that the **words we regularly use to describe our experiences and conditions in life impact and influence our emotional states.** So unknowingly we make our states worse by using and relating high-intensity bad or negative words to our experiences in life. For example using the word 'depressed' for feeling 'down' or 'frustrated'.

You can use words to change how you think, which will change your feelings, decisions and results. Wisely selecting the words we use to describe the experiences in and of our lives can make us feel better thus impacting our decisions and actions. Don't limit your emotional joy with your disabling words! Use the words 'very good' or 'excellent' rather than feeling 'better'.

Our questions determine our thoughts. The questions we ask ourselves, in our head, determine where we focus, how we think, how we feel, and what we decide and/or do. Most people ask ineffective questions of themselves which trigger lame or negative thoughts and negatively affect their results.

These types of questions turn our focus away from what we want and trigger thoughts of what we don't want. They are disempowering and keep us focused on our problems, failures and shortcomings. Basically they bring up things which remind us of what is wrong and what isn't working in our lives.

Effective questions are empowering. They turn our focus to what we want and usually trigger solution oriented thoughts.

For example:

Ineffective questions: Why can't I be happy? How come I never have time for myself? Why do I often feel down?

Effective questions: What can I do to uplift myself? What can I read, listen or watch that would inspire me? Who can I talk to? What places can I visit? Are these feelings a call for change in life? Are there any physical exercises or meditation techniques I can do to feel better?

'I am the greatest; I said that even before I knew I was.' ~ *Muhammad Ali*

Explore yourself

Have you noticed that most of us use extreme words for negative experiences but average words for describing positive experiences, feelings or results?

How many times do you engage in self-criticism versus self-praise in your mind and while talking about yourself with others?

How many times do you complain/blame/moan versus appreciate/praise/thank?

What is your internal battle about? Is it holding you back from moving forward in life?

Your notes

Emotions - what are they making you do?

Most of us experience far more negative emotions, everyday, than positive ones.

In chapter 2 we discussed that the levels of happiness have dropped significantly and it has become an occasional thing! **It is very important to know that we are emotional creatures. All that we do is to fulfil some emotional need.**

The limbic system (or Paleomammalian brain) supports functions including emotion and behaviour but it doesn't understand language. What that means is that the part of your brain which is responsible for your behaviour doesn't understand language, it understands feelings!

Deficiency of vitamins, vital minerals and nutrients can be taken care of with supplements and diet, but what about the deficiency of self-love, self-praise, self-respect? What do you do for the needs like fulfilment, peace of mind or inner-joy? Negative emotions lead to many mental health problems and many physical illnesses.

'To experience positive/healthy emotions you don't need a big house or a nice car or a managerial job or a million dollars in your bank.' ~ Maddy M

Society today is material and fame oriented. We aren't taught that it's the internal-world which matters more than the external; that it's the feelings and emotions which are the fuel of human beings.

The people who themselves didn't know much about creating a high quality life, programmed you to see the world wrong way round. Most of us are concerned about what other people see us as, the clothes we wear, our professional designation, our financial status, the house we live in, the car we drive, the school our kids go to etc.

BUT the truth is that we are 'emotional' creatures. Every action of ours is influenced by our emotions. All that we do for others and for our social image is far less important than experiencing inner-happiness, peace, love and gratitude.

Intellect is not a substitute for emotions. We are conditioned to live for others, to live by the rules of the society which is driven by money, fame and fears!

'People spend a lifetime searching for happiness; looking for peace. They chase idle dreams, addictions, religions, even other people, hoping to fill the emptiness that plagues them. The irony is the only place they ever needed to search was within.'
~ R. L. Anderson

Negative emotions have a purpose too. They tell you something isn't right and must be looked in to.

'Fear and pain should be treated as signals not to close our eyes but to open them wider.' ~ Dr. Nathaniel Branden

'We often try to hide the emotion or run from it. Emotions play a fundamental role in life. They help us to form relationships, experience growth, and evaluate our performance. Besides that, they prompt us to learn and sometimes prompt us to quit, fight, cry, lie, and/or to hide.' ~ Dr. Erik Fisher

It's the emotional issues which people can't handle and they use all sorts of means such as stimulants, self-harm or comfort eating as a solution or distraction.

We have many emotional needs like love, certainty, fulfilment, variety and significance. A part of these needs can be fulfilled by ourselves, however these days most of us try to fulfil these needs completely from outside, hence we become stuck in a loop of showing-off, pleasing others, approval addiction, changing sex partners etc. because most of us have a low self-esteem. Yes we do need some approval or attention from others but a lot of it can come from within us. This is why the fear of rejection is one of the most common in us today! We are begging for love and approval from others.

This type of society, which is full of people with negative/limiting beliefs about themselves, is bound to have more and more mental health patients! Studies show that positive emotions reduce the negative effects of stress on the body (physiology) and improve problem solving skills (decisions leading to results).

'At the end of the day it's not 'what looks good' that matters, it's 'what feels' good.'
~ Maddy M

Explore yourself

When you experience a negative emotion ask: What can I learn from this feeling? Is there something I must resolve?

Your notes

Ten things the most successful, happiest and healthiest people believe in and do

Most of us are either unaware of these or not implementing them effectively.

When I came across these facts I decided to consider, believe in and accept them because these have been, and still are, followed and implemented by the most successful, happy and healthy people. Initially it was hard for me to accept these and to delete my old beliefs but I did and my life changed, literally!

'When presented with a new idea, check your ego at the door and suspend your disbelief. Your ability to open your mind and consider new ideas without fear will propel you to the top faster than anything else.' ~Bill Gove

1) They take responsibility for their lives

Rather than blaming everyone else for the problems in their lives the most successful people say 'I am responsible for my wealth, happiness and health'. They choose to construct their life and control their destiny. They accept themselves and their lives and take responsibility to make it better.

I had every reason to stay mediocre or average, to blame my circumstances, family, country and school but I realised that if I don't take responsibility for my life, accept myself and move forward then who else would! It dawned on me one day that I had to take massive action to make my life better because no one was coming to my rescue. Part of that massive action was my move to the UK.

How are you going to take responsibility for your life?

'In the long run, we shape our lives, and we shape ourselves. The process never ends until we die. And the choices we make are ultimately our own responsibility.'
~Eleanor Roosevelt

'Success on any major scale requires you to accept responsibility. In the final analysis, the one quality that all successful people have is the ability to take responsibility.
~Michael Korda

2) They develop empowering and successful beliefs

Successful people may not be more intelligent or talented than the rest but they believe they can be, do or have anything they want in life. They change attitudes and create habits which help them in making their lives better. They reprogram or recondition their mind for success in every area of their lives. They are not controlled by their fears. They challenge ideas and opinions, rather than just accept them as fact.

I had to get rid of my limiting beliefs and 'lack' programming before I started moving forward in life because they were big blocks which didn't let me see success or happiness. I had fear of failure and my self-confidence was very low. I didn't believe in my abilities. And all these negative beliefs made me stay poor, mediocre, unhappy and hate myself. But when I started to say and believe these three statements things my life started changing for good: 'I can', 'I deserve' and 'I am worthy'.

What happens in your life when you say 'I can', 'I deserve' and 'I am worthy'?

'Our beliefs about ourselves are the most telling factors in determining our level of success and happiness in life.' ~Dr. Wayne Dyer

'The programming that you accept from others, and the conscious and unconscious directives, pictures, feelings and thoughts that you transmit to yourself, will find a place in your own internal control centre. Together, those thoughts and images will continue to create in advance or influence on the spot, every response, attitude and action that will be a part of you and your future.' ~ Dr. Shad Helmsletter

3) They know thoughts become reality

They take responsibility of what they dwell on in their mind. They consciously choose to focus on successful, healthy and happy thoughts. They think big and believe in abundance not lack or scarcity. They are aware of the fact that what they repeat in their mind will become a belief. They keep track of their self-talk including the words they use.

I used to tell myself all kinds of negative things about myself. I used to stop myself from taking action by reminding myself of my failures in the past. I used lame words to describe myself, my abilities and my future. When I explored what I was repeating in my head I was shocked to discover I was reinforcing negative programming and was responsible for my unfulfilled life. I then created affirmations and vision boards to reprogram and focus my mind towards success.

What do you say to yourself? Do you like what you hear?

'They can… because they think they can.' ~Virgil

'Men are not prisoners of fate, but only prisoners of their own minds.'
~Franklin D. Roosevelt

4) They understand the power of emotions

They know managing emotions is crucial for achieving success, happiness and wellness. Thoughts and beliefs trigger emotions so they make sure they have positive and fruitful thoughts as much as possible. They do things which make them happy, which make them laugh, make them feel healthy and which generate the feeling of love. They motivate themselves by emotions related to their dreams, desires and passion rather than by money and material possession.

Changing my beliefs raised my level of self-love. Feeling grateful gives me a sense of fulfilment. Meditation and relaxation gives me peace of mind and working for a purpose and mission gives me happiness. I spend few minutes every day watching or listening to something funny.

'The basic thing is that everyone wants happiness, no one wants suffering. And happiness mainly comes from our own attitude, rather than from external factors. If your own mental attitude is correct, even if you remain in a hostile atmosphere, you feel happy.' ~Dalai Lama

5) They have a clear purpose/vision

They know what they want, why they want it and how to get it. They spend time on setting goals and creating action plans which will create the life of their dreams. They love what they do. They are bold and daring visionaries.

Somewhere within me I wasn't fulfilled. IT wasn't my passion, although it paid me well. But every morning I walked to work with emptiness in me and I just knew this isn't what I am supposed to do. By asking myself questions and by connecting with my inner-self I realised what my true passion was. I then started planning, dreaming and learning the skills required to fulfil and live my purpose.

Do you have a clear vision or purpose for your life? It doesn't need to be world-changing on a global scale – a vision of being the best parent you could be is world-changing enough.

'There is one quality one must possess to win, and that is definiteness of purpose, the knowledge of what one wants and a burning desire to possess it.' ~Napoleon Hill

6) They expect adversity and failure

They are driven to succeed, but unlike the majority they don't avoid mistakes, risks or failure. They don't seek security or comfort. They are criticised but are persistent. They choose discipline over pleasure.

Most people fool themselves by saying 'I work hard' or 'I am quite competent' or 'I am doing whatever I can' when in reality they aren't. The truth is that they have limiting beliefs about money and about what they can achieve or deserve. They want to live the 'rich' life but are unwilling to pay the price.

I was afraid of failure, of taking risk and wanted to have a better life whilst being comfortable. When I realised I was living in delusion I made up my mind to accept discomfort, to take calculated risks and to see the long term rewards. I had a choice to stay in India and live an average life or to migrate and have more freedom and growth opportunities. I had a choice to invest money in personal development or buying a house. I had a choice to keep working a high paying IT job or to work for my passion of helping others to make their life better. And for all these non-linear decisions of mine I was criticised and made fun of by my family, friends and colleagues!!

Warning! A lot of internet marketing, real estate and share trading trainers are selling people 'get rich quick with less effort' courses/products these days. Please be aware. Probably ask them how much time and energy did they spend to reach where they are ;-). The truth is that there is no 'quick' to getting rich!

'If you don't step out of your comfort zone and face your fears, the number of situations that make you uncomfortable will keep growing.' ~Theo Pistorius

'To succeed in life one must have determination and must be prepared to suffer during the process. If one isn't prepared to suffer during adversities, I don't really see how he can be successful.' ~ Gary Player

7) They don't look for immediate rewards

This one goes hand in hand with no. 6 above. Unlike others they don't believe that compensation should instantly follow any effort. They know it can take years to manifest their ultimate vision, dream or goals. They focus on gratification which lasts rather than instant pleasure.

It took me almost two years to settle down in the UK. I could have started practicing life coaching, hypnotherapy or NLP soon after I completed the course but I first implemented it in my life so I could walk my talk. I could have taken a two-day course on public speaking and started my seminars but I opted for a year long course which is taught by the top 1% of speakers in the world. Believe it or not it can take the best professionals up to a year to prepare an hour long comedy show, speech or music performance!!

Can you delay the gratification of an instant success for a longer term more sustainable outcome?

'The key to everything is patience. You get the chicken by hatching the egg, not by smashing it.' ~Arnold H. Glasgow

8) They have coaches and mentors. They are ever-ready learners.

They are committed to never ending personal and professional growth. They attend seminars and/or workshops and read books. They believe in working smarter not harder so they learn from the mentors or role-models that are the best in their fields which also helps them accelerate their performance. They have coaches for different areas of their lives. They invest time and money in getting better. For them failure is an opportunity to learn and grow.

I haven't stopped learning since I attended a personal development seminar a few years ago. I read books, I attend personal and professional development seminars often, I have three coaches for different areas of my life and I constantly apply this learning and suggest it to my clients.

Are you still green and growing, willing to learn?

'The most successful among us are not always the class valedictorians, but they are the best self-educated people on the planet.' ~unknown

9) They take care of their physical fitness, nutrition and relaxation

They understand physical activity is a must and it has numerous benefits both emotionally, mentally and physically. They consciously choose what they eat, when they eat and how much they eat. They make time to relax their body and mind because they know we aren't robots.

I had no clue about nutrition and was very lazy until a few years ago. I used to spend a lot of my time watching TV and chatting on the phone. I was surprised to see the effects of regular exercise on my mind and body. My immune system is far better since I started taking care of my diet.

Do you take care of your body – or expect it to take care of you?

> *'Exercise is king, nutrition is queen, but together you have the entire kingdom!'*
> *~Jack Lalanne*

10) They forgive and are grateful

They know a lack of forgiveness can block dreams and goals from manifesting in every area of life.

> *'We achieve inner health only through forgiveness - the forgiveness not only of others but also of ourselves'* ~ *Joshua Liebman*

They are grateful for what they have. This not only gives them a sense of fulfilment it also increases their self-esteem and confidence. A biological benefit of this is that the brain releases useful chemicals during this process of expressing gratitude.

Until I went through the process of forgiving others and myself I was sabotaging my peace of mind, happiness and success. I was full of blames, complains, resentment and lack. Being grateful for what I already have and what I achieve in my day-to-day life gives me inner joy.

Are you grateful for everything you have, everything you have achieved and everything that is yet to come?

'It is necessary to cultivate the habit of being grateful for every good thing that comes to you, and to give thanks continuously.' - Wallace Wattles

Your notes

Practical tips and techniques to make your life better

Get started on changing your life for the better right now.

Maybe this is the first time you have really thought about yourself or looked deeply into your life and it may feel weird but if you want to make your life better then you will have to evaluate your assumptions, beliefs, values and priorities. It will be worth the investment.

Today is a good day to start knowing your 'self' and to plan for betterment of your life. When you understand how your beliefs, emotions and thoughts are affecting your attitude, decisions, actions and results, and you change the ones that aren't working for you, then you will see a difference in every area of your life.

Your life is YOUR responsibility

The first step is to become aware of your 'self'. If you have been pondering the Explore Yourself questions in the previous chapters you will already be becoming aware of your 'self', your thoughts and beliefs and your consequential actions.

You'll have started to realise that...

- No miracle may happen.
- No God's angel may come to rescue you.
- You probably won't find Aladdin's magic lamp on a street.
- No one else will take action on your behalf.
- Just wishing or dreaming will not make your life better...

...but taking action will!

A big breakthrough which jolted me out of my trance/illusion/helplessness was realising that nothing will change if I don't take responsibility for my life; if I don't look into my life and if I don't take action to make it better.

'Your time is limited, so don't waste it living someone else's life. Don't be trapped by dogma - which is living with the results of other people's thinking. Don't let the noise of other's opinions drown out your own inner voice. And most important, have the courage to follow your heart and intuition. They somehow already know what you truly want to become. Everything else is secondary.' ~ Steve Jobs

Live consciously

Living consciously means being aware and being accountable for where you are in regards to your goals and targets for every area of your life. Self-evaluation and getting feedback from external sources to evaluate the results you are getting, admitting your mistakes and looking for solutions to rectify them. Persevering in adverse situations. Having an open mind to receive new information and willingness to edit or delete old beliefs, rules, habits and assumptions and adding new ones for betterment of your life. Believing that learning is a never ending process. Understanding your needs, purpose, values etc.

Most of us are so lost in the past, watching our same old painful movie again and again, that we forget the solutions exist but they do and we have all the resources we need to find them. Try asking yourself some simple questions to provoke your subconscious into finding those solutions for you.

What can I do to make my condition/situation/life better?

What have I achieved by cursing my past, by hating myself and by blaming people and circumstances?

What can I do to create the life of my dreams in the present and future?

'Will you look back in your life and say 'I wish I had' or 'I'm glad I did'?'
~ Zig Ziglar

Become aware of your thought patterns

Your thoughts become your physical reality!

We live in the world of our thoughts all day long. The amount of happiness, success, love, peace and fulfilment you experience and achieve depends on the nature and quality of your thoughts. **The good news is that you can make a conscious choice as to what thoughts you think (what you focus on) and which actions you take (or not take) and to override negative, limiting or disempowering thoughts.**

Take a moment and make a list of people, media and events which influence your day-to-day thoughts.

Many personal development and spiritual gurus suggest that we decrease the time we spend on watching or listening to the daily news because it is full of negative stories; especially if you watch or listen to it every morning then you feed your subconscious mind with a breakfast full of negative stuff and you probably think about some of that throughout the day.

Initially, you may find it difficult to keep track of every thought and they may keep coming back but with practice you will become more aware of them and then can change them for something more helpful and positive if they are unhelpful or disempowering thoughts.

'It is mental discipline to keep certain thoughts out of your head and put certain thoughts in your head. You have conscious control over that. It takes practice and repetition.' ~ 1996 Gold Medal Swimmer

'With self-discipline most anything is possible.' ~ Theodore Roosevelt

If you need help to identify and control the thoughts that are not serving you and are blocking your path to your success and happiness, then contact me for one to one coaching (success@bulletproofbelief.com).

Take control of your self-talk, inner-gremlin or inner-critics

Have you ever questioned your inner-critic? Do you trust it?

What do you say to yourself about:

- Your identity and abilities (appearance, worthiness, competence and intelligence)
- What you deserve in each area of your life
- What would your future be? What are the possibilities in different areas of life?
- What do you say to yourself during difficult situations or while trying something new?
- What does your inner critic say about the life in general? (life is a battle, full of problems, sucks, hell)
- What kind of self-talk do you usually have for others and for the world around you?

In many situations, the only thing you can control is your own response. Changing self-talk from negative to positive is an excellent way to manage that response. We weren't taught that the words we regularly use to describe our experiences and conditions in life impact and influence our emotional states. Use your words wisely and kindly, as you would to your best friend.

Stop blaming yourself. Stop regretting. Stop focusing on the past. Stop listening to people who don't support you and who aren't experiencing happiness, success, peace and fulfilment for themselves. Stop labelling yourself as 'unlucky'. What would your best friend say to you? Ask them! And be your own best friend too.

Our questions determine our thoughts

The questions we ask ourselves, in our head, determine where we focus, how we think, how we feel, and what we decide and/or do. So it's time to ask ourselves better questions.

Try asking questions like these:

Everyone deserves happiness. When am I going to allow myself the happiness I deserve?

How much more am I capable of?

When will I reach my perfect weight, now I am committed to doing what it takes to get there?

How could I find a perfect soul mate? What is really likeable about me?

What could I do right now to make myself feel better and beat this depressed feeling?

Your subconscious starts working to validate what you ask yourself. It looks for evidence and finds references to back it up. So asking questions like 'What can I do to make my condition/situation/ life better?' immediately gets your subconscious working on solutions rather than finding more evidence for the problem.

Evaluate/Challenge your beliefs

YOU need to get better before your life gets better so create a better mindset. Success starts within and stems from your beliefs. Happiness comes from within and depends on your beliefs.

A sad truth is that most of us don't know what we really believe! We don't know what is holding us back. Beliefs have the power to make us successful or not, happy or depressed, loving or criminal. Negative or limiting beliefs limit our ability to achieve the life we desire. Very few of us examine our beliefs critically. So here is an opportunity to do just that.

'It's not the events of our lives that shape us, but our beliefs as to what those events mean.' ~ Tony Robbins

On a scale of 1-10 check your <u>worth levels</u> by asking: Am I worthy of...

- A lot of money/luxury
- Being loved
- Being promoted, getting more business
- Happiness

On a scale of 1-10 check your <u>deserving levels</u> by asking: Do I deserve...

- A lot of money/to be rich
- An abundance of love
- Happiness
- A fit body

On a scale of 1-10 check your <u>ability levels</u> by asking: Am I capable of...

- Earning lots of money
- Attracting the right soul mate
- Getting promotion, handling more/larger business

Pick up an area to explore. Write down the challenges/problems you are facing. Then ask yourself, which beliefs of mine are responsible for this? What fears do I have in that area, that are stopping me from achieving desired results?

In detail write down:

What are these beliefs costing me emotionally, physically and/or financially?

What are their negative effects on my relationships and/or profession?

Start writing the beliefs you would like to replace the old ones with. Usually the opposite of the old beliefs works best. Work through each belief and list the benefits that the new beliefs will have. What feelings will the new ones generate?

Be honest and be willing to take the responsibility of your life from this very moment. **Your results will change only when the old false beliefs are replaced with the ones which will serve you for good.** Utilising your power to choose your beliefs consciously and intentionally can improve the quality of every area of your life.

> *'When you doubt your power, you give power to your doubt.'*
> *~ Honore de Balzac*

> *'Within you right now is the power to do things you never dreamed possible. This power becomes available to you just as soon as you can change your beliefs.'*
> *~ Maxwell Maltz*

Create your goals

Setting goals without changing your self-talk and beliefs will not work in the long term. Remember, most of us sabotage our success because of our beliefs, fears and assumptions. Also, our subconscious mind keeps us away from pain hence it stops us from taking actions which are outside our comfort zone. We must reprogram it to move forward or to take risk or to be uncomfortable.

Emotions create motion. They motivate you to take action. So make sure you write how you will feel after achieving or during the process of achieving a goal.

'Many people fail in life, not for lack of ability or brains or even courage but simply because they have never organized their energies around a goal.' ~ *Elbert Hubbard*

Assess where you are in life right now and where you want to go. Here is an easy formula for creating a goal:

I will (goal + performance measure) by (specific actions)

Example: I will lose 10 pounds in two months by running on a treadmill for half an hour six days a week.

'Whatever you do, you need courage. Whatever course you decide upon, there is always someone to tell you that you are wrong. There are always difficulties arising that tempt you to believe your critics are right. To map out a course of action and follow it to an end requires some of the same courage that a soldier needs. Peace has its victories, but it takes brave men and women to win them.' ~ *Ralph Waldo Emerson*

Action is a must

Now that you are aware of what is stopping you and you have changed some of those thoughts, beliefs and self talk, there are no more excuses to stay stuck in your lack of confidence, your financial struggle, be overweight, have bad relationships or whatever difficulty you are having in your life.

It's time to break free. Stop avoiding and start creating.

You deserve to be rich. You deserve to live a happy life. You deserve peace of mind. You deserve your respect. You deserve loving relationships. And YES, it's all possible.

'Knowing is not enough; we must apply. Willing is not enough; we must do.'
~ *Johann Wolfgang von Goethe*

Most of us know what we want BUT we don't do much about it! But that isn't you anymore is it? You know that there is NO quick fix for it; that the **power of change is within you and only you can make that change;**

that choice is always there and you have complete control over what you choose to think and do.

'This life is yours. Take the power to choose what you want to do and do it well. Take the power to love what you want in life and love it honestly. Take the power to walk in the forest and be a part of nature. Take the power to control your own life. No one else can do it for you. Take the power to make your life happy.'
~ Susan Polis Schutz

If there was one action that you could take immediately to instantly change the quality of your emotions and feelings every day of your life then what would that be?

Your Notes

You Were Born Great. With A Mind Which Had No Limiting Beliefs Which Means You Could Be, Have, Become or Feel Anything You Wish.

You were programmed to be average.

You were programmed to feel unworthy.

You were programmed to compete/be perfectionist

You were programmed to love others more than yourself

You learned to experience more negative emotions than positive

You can choose to stay here

OR YOU CAN CHOOSE TO MOVE HERE

You Can Be Rich, Happy, Fit, Confident, Proud, Adventurous, Joyful, Love-Full, Funny, at Peace...

and Live the Life Of Your Dreams.

© Maddy M

Congratulations!

You have now taken those first great steps towards living the life you dream of and deserve. Your good wolf's belly will be growing in contentment for finally you are feeding it with positive beliefs, empowering self-talk and joyous emotions.

When you need help to take the next steps to happiness, fulfilment, joy, wealth and wellness, then contact me and I will be your guide. Whether you would like me to work with you as your personal coach or you would prefer my home study guides (or both!), I will be very happy to help you on your journey.

I wish you a Wealthier, Happier, Love-filled, Healthier and Peaceful life!

Maddy M.

Maddy M ☺

IT'S MY CHOICE *by Maddy M*

I get a gift every morning, the gift of a new day,

It's up to me whether I make it bright, joyful or grey.

I can choose to be Happy, Successful and Content,

Or dishonour it with worry, anger or resent.

The next steps with Maddy M

One to One Coaching

I will help you to change your limiting beliefs, thoughts and self talk, and support you to set goals, so YOU can

- ✓ **Progress** in your **career** or business
- ✓ **Gain confidence** and improve your self-image
- ✓ **Feel good** by achieving your **ideal body shape** and
- ✓ Have **fulfilling relationships** and have **more time** for your family and yourself
- ✓ **Achieve** your **goals** and follow through your intentions
- ✓ **Increase** your **income** to **enjoy** the luxuries you wish
- ✓ **Have a better** attitude. Make better decisions.
- ✓ Be a **good parent** (ensure your child's happy and successful life)
- ✓ **Be in control** of your reactions

When you are ready to develop your own bullet-proof self beliefs, then email: **success@bulletproofbelief.com**
Or visit: **www.bulletproofbelief.com**

'Bullet–Proof Your Self Belief' Home Study Course

Would you like to feel better about yourself than ever before? Would you like to see yourself producing better results? Would you like to feel more fulfilled in your work, your relationships and your life?

My new home study course Bullet-Proof Your Self Belief will help you work on your beliefs, emotions, thoughts and self-talk, and help you achieve every goal you set yourself *without fail.*

The home study course will help you get rid of:

- ✖ Limiting/negative beliefs
- ✖ Fear of failure
- ✖ Low self-esteem
- ✖ Lack of self-confidence
- ✖ A feeling of not being good enough
- ✖ Negative self image
- ✖ Feeling 'unlucky'
- ✖ Procrastination
- ✖ Lack of fulfilment and peace of mind
- ✖ Negative attitude

You will learn in detail:

- ➢ How to change your limiting beliefs
- ➢ How to create new empowering beliefs and techniques to really embed and support them
- ➢ How to change and manage your emotions
- ➢ How to change your self-talk and daily thoughts to support your new beliefs
- ➢ How to set goals in such a way that you can't fail to achieve them

The home study course will help you understand WHY you have problems or barriers in any given area of life and provide you with PROVEN tools and techniques to help you get rid of problems and make your life better. The course provides both the theory behind all these techniques and why they work, and exercises for you to put these techniques into practise for yourself, bullet-proofing your self-belief.

On completing the home study course you will have rock solid, bullet-proof self belief so that you can

✓ Achieve any goal you set (e.g. for increasing your income, achieving your ideal body shape, building high self esteem or anything else)
✓ Feel confident about yourself
✓ Make better decisions for yourself
✓ Feel good about yourself and your achievements
✓ Focus on the positive things in your life and manifest more of them
✓ Be more of the person you want to be
✓ Take control of your emotional reactions

Get yours now!!!

To get started on bullet-proofing your self-belief with the home study course go to **www.bulletproofbelief.com** or email **homestudy@bulletproofbelief.com.** Quote this code and you'll receive **$20** off the purchase price! The code is: **happyme247.**

Join Maddy M

For more valuable information, book updates and inspiring quotes and discussions: **www.facebook.com/maddymfanpage**

Read and subscribe for more valuable information on life, my radio interviews and videos on my blog: **www.bulletproofbelief.com**

For updates, inspirational quotes and more:
https://twitter.com/coachmaddym

Media
For media information and media appearances
email: **media@bulletproofbelief.com**

Comments on the book: email: **book@bulletproofbelief.com**

Maddy M

Bullet Proof Belief

CPSIA information can be obtained at www.ICGtesting.com
Printed in the USA
235620LV00010B/107/P

9 781456 585082